C000049852

Compilation copyright © 1997 Lion Publishing
This edition copyright © 1997 Lion Publishing
Text copyright © 1997 Tom Wright
The author asserts the moral right to be
identified as the author of this work

Published by
Lion Publishing plc
Sandy Lane West, Oxford, England
ISBN 0 7459 3838 8
First edition 1997
10 9 8 7 6 5 4 3 2 1
A catalogue record for this book is available
from the British Library
Printed and bound in Singapore

Commissioning editor: Meryl Doney
Project editor: Nina Webley
Book designer: Nicholas Rous
Jacket designer: Jonathan Roberts
Studio photography: Andrew Whittuck

A Moment

o f

Prayer

Tom Wright

LION
Giftlines

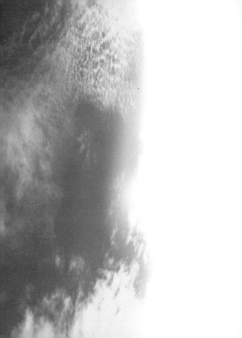

Contents

Introduction

These books are designed to help you explore the presence of God. You can open them at random. Or you can work through, perhaps, a page a day.

The books move in a sequence. The first, *A Moment of Prayer*, starts at the centre, and looks at the words of prayer. The second, *A Moment of Quiet*, explores what happens when we stop talking and listen. The third,

A *Moment of Peace*, is about
reconciliation between God
and ourselves. The final volume,
A Moment of Celebration, is about
worshipping God, alone or with
others.

Prayer is a universal human
experience, yet it remains mysterious.
These reflections are meant to nudge
the reader into prayer, perhaps from
unfamiliar angles. Using words in

prayer may help. So may (for some, not all) 'praying in tongues', the special languages of the Spirit. What matters is practising being in God's presence, and being part of the movement of his love reaching into the world. My aim has been to open doors and point through them. Which ones you go through is up to you—and God, of course.

'There's no point in spending
time in Jerusalem if we never
get to see the King's face.'

Prayer is...

Prayer

is...

faith asking.

Prayer is...

hope

waiting.

Prayer is...
love embracing.

Prayer is...

me being me

in the presence of

God being God.

Prayer is...
God being God
in me
being me.

Prayer is...

the catalyst *that means*

the experiment will

work at last.

Prayer is...

a glass of wine
poured into a
bowl of water,
suffusing it with
its gentle colour.

Prayer

Prayer...
opens the
locked gate
into the
rose garden.

nor superior.

Prayer...
helps us to grow to
our proper height,

neither inferior

P r a y e r . . .
cleans the mirror in which I
look at   myself, so
that I   can   see
myself as others see me, or even
(God help me) as God sees me.

Prayer...

removes the spectacles of pride
and fear through which I
normally look at everyone else,
and helps me
see them as
God sees
them.

Prayer...
opens up the
old wound
which hasn't healed
right, eases in the
ointment, and helps
it to heal at last.

Prayer...
takes the
tangled ball of
wool and gently
untangles it,
without
snapping it or
cutting it.

Prayer...

is the most

human thing

we can do—

and the most

divine.

I pray

because

I pray because...

God always intended

to bring humans in on the act,

without letting them

get proud in the process.

I pray because...
I often need to tell
someone things and
there's no one else
I can tell them to.

I pray because...

I often need

to be told things

that no one else

will tell me.

I pray because...
The natural focus of the
sight of a newborn child is
the distance between the
mother's breast and the
mother's eyes.

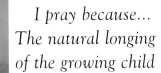

I pray because...
The natural longing
of the growing child
is to
spend
time
with her
father.

Praying in

Praying in words...
because words not only
articulate praise—
they become praise.

w o r d s

Praying in words...
because words not only describe
beauty—they become beauty.

Praying
in words...
because
words
not
only
clothe
prayer—

they
become
prayer.

Praying in words...

because until I've said it

I don't always know what

I was thinking or feeling.

Praying in words...

because God
treats us as
children, not
     as pet animals.

Praying in words...
because without words
ritual can
become magic.

Praying in words...

because without words

silence can

become meaningless.

Praying in words...
because without words
we can fool ourselves
with half-truths.

*Praying in words...
because when God
came among us,
he came as the
Word Incarnate.*

Praying

in

tongues

Praying   *in*

tongues...

is   a   lover's

language:

nonsense   to

outsiders,

but ideal for

intimacy.

Praying in tongues...
is a way of saying
more than we have
words to say.

Praying in tongues...

is a way of

getting in touch with things

I didn't know

were going on inside me.

Praying in tongues...

is a little running stream,

flowing from the

still lake of God's grace

into the

deep ocean of God's love.

Praying in tongues...
is the flutter of a flag
in the breeze,

showing that the King
is in residence.

Praying in tongues...
enables me to pray
for someone
when I don't know
what to pray for.

Praying in tongues...

 is what sometimes

happens when God's love

takes your breath away

 and you're left with

God's breath instead.

Moments of

A moment of prayer...

when the pain is

sharper even

than I'd feared.

prayer

A   moment   of

p r a y e r . . .

when   sudden

j   o   y

washes over me

like   a   tidal

w   a   v   e.

A moment of prayer...
when I realize I've
stepped off
the cliff of
my own
resources,
and without
God's help I'm lost.

Blessings

May God give you the gift to enjoy
his presence, to hear his voice,
to let him hear yours,
and to grow in his love.

May God give you the gift

of praying for his world,

his work, his children,

and his *future.*